SMALL-TOWN TERROR

SMALL-TOWN TERROR

T.J. RAVENSCROFT

CONTENTS

1 Disclaimer — 1
2 Introduction — 3
3 Chapter 1: The Abductions — 7
4 Chapter 2: The Investigation — 11
5 Chapter 3: The Discovery — 15
6 Chapter 4: The Trial — 19
7 Chapter 5: The Aftermath — 23
8 Conclusion — 27
9 References — 29

Copyright © 2024 by T.J. Ravenscroft
All rights reserved. No part of this book may be reproduced in any manner whatsoever without written permission except in the case of brief quotations embodied in critical articles and reviews.
First Printing, 2024

CHAPTER 1

Disclaimer

The content in this book is intended for informational and entertainment purposes only. While every effort has been made to ensure the accuracy of the information presented, the author and publisher make no representations or warranties of any kind, express or implied, about the completeness, accuracy, reliability, suitability, or availability with respect to the content of this book.

The views and opinions expressed in this book are those of the author and do not necessarily reflect the official policy or position of any individual, company, or organization mentioned. Any resemblance to actual persons, living or dead, or actual events is purely coincidental.

This book is not intended to defame, libel, or slander any person, company, or organization. All references to individuals, companies, products, and brands are for illustrative purposes only, and no affiliation with or endorsement by them is intended or implied.

The author and publisher disclaim any responsibility for any actions or outcomes resulting from the application of information contained in this book. Readers should seek professional advice or conduct their own research when making decisions based on the content provided.

All rights reserved. No part of this book may be reproduced, distributed, or transmitted in any form or by any means, including photocopying, recording, or other electronic or mechanical methods, without the prior written permission of the author, except in the case of brief quotations embodied in critical reviews and certain other non-commercial uses permitted by copyright law.

CHAPTER 2

Introduction

Larry Gene Bell cast a long, dark shadow in the small town of Lugoff, South Carolina kidnapping and killing two local girls in 1985. His young victims were abducted off the streets near their homes, held captive for days, sexually molested, and then strangled. Valencia Williams was 14 and his neighbor Sharon Faye Smith was only 9. Despite the summertime tragedy, the community quickly weathered up the windows of their homes and local institutions sprang for yellow and black ribbons – in Sharon's favorite color and Valencia's school colors. The visual display united the town, representing a collective hope for the safe return of the girls. Days into their searches, Valencia and Sharon were found dead by the side of a dirt road sixty miles from home.

The culprit turned out to be a local man and one well-known to the Smiths: Larry Gene Bell. A father and husband, Bell was a known drifter who occasionally worked as a laborer. He lived in a rented house with his wife and two youngest sons, plus the oldest boy from Bell's first marriage. Charming and goal-oriented, friends knew Bell for his landscaping prowess and endless self-improvement projects. Trained as a nurse, Bell's points of pride were bridging the gap between small-town medicine and big city innovations and warding off necrosis in his patients. He was small-town famous for successfully treating numerous snakebites. Fewer people knew about his anger or his criminal history, a problematic combination. The crime stunned America.

Background of Larry Gene Bell

Larry Gene Bell was a lonely man who had always had problems with the ladies. Born in the parish seat of Woodville in 1949, Bell was the second of Elbert and Myrtle Bell's two sons. The Bell family had deep roots in Wilkinson County, the most heavily forested part of a heavily forested state. Rapidly depopulated by a steady drain to bigger places, Woodville and the surrounding area had effectively become the pockets of emptiness in a densely populated web of pine trees. Elbert Bell worked as a farm laborer, a truck driver, and a section hand for the Canadian National Railroad by the time his sons were born. Notwithstanding his own flinty marginality, Elbert had high hopes for both of his boys, especially for Larry, the younger of the two.

By the time hardworking Bell père died of heart failure in 1961, having never improved his seventh-grade education, Dennis—the elder brother—had begun to give up on young Larry. "I told him to go [off] and make something of himself," Dennis said later. But bright and attractive in his daydreams and morose introspection, Larry Bell appeared to the people who meant the most to him as lazy, shiftless, and fatalistically morbid. Most Vergilians await only the arrival of death. At Edison, however, Larry Bell openly twitted Death the bellboy and once embarked on a childishly overblown protest of the Empire for postponing an audience with the Emperor. Later, of course, he took on the role with terrifying gusto.

Setting the Stage: Small-Town America
Small-town America, small-town life—these are phrases and stereotypes that are easily recognizable to many and reviled by many more. A Norman Rockwellian vision that captures an idyllic and simple life, chipped away by change, loss, and modernization. Small towns vary widely, but whatever the circumstances, all have a combination of "homogeneity, loyalty to family, belief in local solutions for local problems," and upward social mobility. Bell's crimes took place in a one-stoplight town, a community of 2,000 located on a tidal bay. It was isolated despite burgeoning urban disasters that surrounded the community in every direction. It was a typical southern town but bifurcated by race—a Jordan's poisoned utopia.

At the time of Bell's arrest, the 83rd largest market in the country, depending on string-ologies of chicken, textiles, and shrimps. It was a place where a man's business card might proclaim "Husband, Father, Grandfather, Fence Erector." The community's recreational activities included coon hunting with dogs and a half-dozen Baptist and Methodist churches to keep the children good on Sunday school and home economics instead of sex education, labeling apples—prepared with biscuits and a spoon of mayonnaise—for the junior chamber of commerce annual banquet. Two traffic lights guarded the main intersection; there was one school where its 600 elementary, middle, and high school students built coral reefs in tabletop fish tanks for displays at a career fair. Baby boomers dominate the town's population, constituting 35 percent of residents. A community where families teetered on the edge, with 15 percent below the poverty line and 20 percent elderly over the age of 60.

For more than a year, the world's media descended and stayed on Beaufort County's biggest news story, parked in parks and by the courthouse and jail, and on the screens of America's 2nd largest newspaper, Charleston, SC's The Post and Courier. But what happens after the media goes home, after the world has moved on?

CHAPTER 3

Chapter 1: The Abductions

Ed M. reflected that the night of June 7, 1985, had seemed much hotter than usual. Ed was almost midway through the graveyard shift at the Dutch Oven bakery. He also ran the Nightwatchman club in Chesnee, and Shari Faye's family was among his regulars. He was dimly aware that he'd have to make a pot of fresh coffee for when they heard the news. It was just after 2 a.m. when the phone rang at Trendline, a research and marketing company in Chesnee on East Cherokee Street. Janice R., who was just starting her shift, had decided to call home. That ringing brought cries for help.

Janice took the call every mother dreads. She stayed calm and got as much information as possible before hanging up the telephone and screaming for her husband, son, and sister to "Grab your lights," she told them. Janice's daughter sat at the computer mostly staring blankly at the dark screen and slowly trying to compose herself the way she had been taught during seven years of weekly piano lessons. At 6:36 a.m., a pair of Exper-Lube workers called the police to tell them about a gray car parked in the sand pits. A walk around the vehicle revealed tires imprinted with the letters FIRESTONE BANKS. It was the distinctive coil that would soon bring the FBI to the Bible Belt. He waved behind him to the second patrol car coming. A white Peugeot 505 station wagon swooped in behind the other car. Officers raced toward it. Knocking gently on darkened windows, they looked for someone awake amid the "HELP US" written in the mist with a fingertip.

The Disappearances of Shari Faye Smith and Debra May Helmick
On March 5, 1985, a young girl in town named Debra May Helmick disappeared on her way to school. Her remaining family was enamored with Bell and his escape from death row in 1987. When Bell was finally caught again in December of 1985, Rev. Helmick wrote him a letter in support of his doing anything he could to stay alive and prove his innocence. Within the year, Larry Gene Bell would abduct Shari Faye Smith, the daughter of Greg and Dee Smith. Its impact on her family was almost unparalleled. In a few short days, any and all perceptions of safety had been quickly and soundly shattered. Mrs. Smith was a fanatic about following standards on how children should be raised. On the morning of April 4, 1985, Shari Faye Smith disappeared on her way to place the deposit form her paper route earnings into a drop box on the front apron of First Citizens Bank.

A brief article appeared in the Union Daily Times located on the front page, but for Lance, nothing much changed. After all, when Shari disappeared, the police had driven up Banberry and put a road block up so nothing could come in or go out. They had even questioned the workers at the firehouse and searched the Bullington house next to the station, including the smell in the car the Smiths had borrowed. Allen Ray, the man from Lockhart who'd been seen talking with Shari May Smith, had answered the deputies' questions and allowed them to question his landlady, Frances Calofix. He had no alibi and had been let go because they had no reason to hold him, but he would always be in their minds, the "culprit who got away" in this story. No one had seen Shari walk down the hill toward the bank, and the pick up van the Smiths had bought had not been seen at all until her empty lunch box, undisturbed earnings, and surrounding puzzle pieces of an unsolvable crime made it into the hands of Union PD, who began the search for gangly, dark-haired individuals in light blue bellbottoms with houndstooth checks.

CHAPTER 4

Chapter 2: The Investigation

Law enforcement used every resource available to find Bell and to unravel the mystery and the terror surrounding the events that afternoon of September 27. Bell was one of two suspects in the recent abduction of two young girls who disappeared while riding their bicycles in broad daylight on County Line Road. Local privacy was continuously disrupted by the needs of law enforcement demanding interviews, affidavits, polygraphs, dental charts, dental examinations, hairbrushes, fingerprints, missing person reports, and photographs of victims riding bicycles and posing in their prom dresses and caps and gowns at graduation, mementos of happier times.

Hysteria and rumor fed fear. Everyone was suspect, neighbors watched neighbors, calls bombarded 4 different state and local law enforcement agencies. Roadblocks were assembled quickly to screen passing vehicles, promising leads came and went with a rapidity that begged despair and revolt. Children stranded at nearby schools were picked up by frantic parents while parents and police searched neighborhoods and garages. Reporters held anxious vigil over the police scanner, punctuating the broadcasts with calls to 911 for news that held the police amazed and ultimately suspect in the investigation. The public's clamor for news came to focus on one issue as well, the trial and probable execution of whoever was involved in the death of 9-year-old Shari. Her prosecutor would argue in Bell's trial that Shari was sexually assaulted and suffered an agonizing death. The public also wanted an instant, positive ID of the victims. Bell's arrest, conducted in quiet silence at a house a few miles away from the girl's grim prison, did little to satisfy America's need for quick justice and closure, but it did restore York County's self-image as a safe place in which to rear children.

Law Enforcement Response
It wasn't until Debra May Helmick was missing for several days that police began to suspect something more troubling was responsible for the disappearances. A team of FBI agents, led by Dennis L. Miller, invaded the small office of the Lexington County Sheriff's Department and set up with an emphasis on the computer. The office was still operating as normal as they mapped out and began their investigation. Despite Larry Bell's insistence that Helmick was a runaway, neither FBI agents nor local police had received any evidence to suggest this was the case. They began to work on the assumption that Helmick had been abducted but, more optimistically, might still be alive.

The missing-persons report said Helmick had last been seen at the Hedrick residence on her way home. So, until Bell's murders and letters to news organizations some three weeks later, authorities presumed Helmick's abductor had known her or at least her family. More than two dozen Lexington police officers and sheriff's deputies searched a fifty-square-mile area between the Hedrick home and the Helmick house in the four days from 12 May. Bloodhounds, borrowed from the Dorchester County Sheriff's Department, had failed to pick up a scent from the J & B intersection to the Helmick residence along the 2.2 miles. Pills also failed to turn up any clues to Debra's whereabouts after Larry's arrest. The gas station at the intersection of Routes 6 and 285 in Lexington County was searched unsuccessfully, as were several ditches on Route 6 approaching Lexington, S.C.

CHAPTER 5

Chapter 3: The Discovery

At 11 a.m. on Sept. 29, 1985, Kirk Price was drinking coffee and waiting for friends at a hunting cabin in Sumter National Forest when he found a piece of skull. It was debris in the yard of the home on Prickly Pear Road, where the potential evidence did not exactly seem out of place. A hard rain could unearth hidden belongings, deposit them all over the land. But this debris seemed important, so he unwrapped his shredded shirt and swiped it across the top of the coffee can. Satisfied, he set it upside down off the slab porch and got up.

A half hour later, Jack Logan and Jerry Price arrived. They volunteered to help the library board member friend and his son set up at this cabin 45 minutes southwest of Columbia, in order to take target practice together. Old newspapers wallowed in the yard, brown like haystacks bloated in a pond. Logan's recollection of that day is difficult to recall because he did not yet realize how historic it was. "We didn't know, none of us," Logan says. We is Logan and I, sitting on dates of newspapers and magazines being reconstructed in his memory three decades later in Little Mountain, Newberry County. Neither of us knew, what's more, that since that fateful day, Logan and his family have been keeping a watch over The Cove. At the time, "we picked that paper up and threw it aside. We didn't think about it." In Chapter 3 of "Small-Town Terror: The Larry Gene Bell Story and the Crime That Stunned America," Free Times staff writer Chris Trainor narrates the events that led to this discovery and immediate aftermath.

Finding the Victims' Bodies

MAY 29, 1985: For the first time since the day they disappeared, Debra May Helmick and Kimberley Dawn Gholl were the focus of the people who had come to know of their stories through the often frightening and sometimes contradictory stories of a man called Larry Gene Bell. Within a few moments of entering the barn, the men from the Coroner's office had identified the second body. The earlier suppositions had been accurate. There was something wrong with the smaller left foot and the long, narrow bones that protruded from the decaying legs had offered no indication of the deceased's height. It was the gold cross with three emerald chips that provided the confirmation. In the nearest corner of the long barn her father and her brother and other family members sat waiting and hoping for news from the door. Outside, other officials were performing the delicate and slow task of removing the bodies from the ground, shovelful by cautious shovelful. The entire process would take more than an hour.

Carolina Field Ledford was only 24 years old. And she had spent the past twelve days being accused in the Lawngate by a man named Larry Gene Bell, a man who had no responsibility to offer her anything except a safe passage as he came to tell the lawmen where to find her children. As the news broke over the gathered crowd, she was surrounded by family members and as the news fell over the gathered crowd, she and others had waited for the news in the whitewood and dusty barn with the long fields of yellow stubbled corn fields that were waited in one-panel splays against the large wooden planks of the barn's old-fashioned and wooden-slat walls.

CHAPTER 6

Chapter 4: The Trial

Although the potential jurors did their best to be impartial and not be influenced by the anticrime fever prevailing in South Carolina, it is hard to judge which potential jurors could have blocked out the hype surrounding Bell's capture, the blizzard of newspaper publicity, the radio and TV reports, and the defensive crouch of everyone connected with what may have been his trial. Two possibilities did exist. The first was to try to find a qualified jury from another part of the state or from some other state entirely. Such a move, however, would not only be enormously expensive, it would be risky because these jurors would have to have been screened effectively to make sure the Debra Helmick hustlers of Bell country had not shifted their allegiance to the accused murderer. The second and best possibility was to bring in objective, intelligent jurors from the general area, to let the prospective jurors become naturalized citizens of the jury, as it were, so that they at least appeared to be more or less above it all on day one of the trial itself. It might work if the judge and defense didn't blow it. The defense had been trying to find a way to have the trial delayed, presumably to give the fury over the Helmick murder more time to wane. Bell himself had suggested to John Bell that perhaps the best move right now was "to lay low and keep cool until this thing blows over." But Burnett said he was ready to go to trial, and John Bell agreed with him wholeheartedly. So the trial was scheduled.

In courtroom face-offs between sides following different strategies, the dynamics can be as revealing, as human, as anything anywhere. Few if any criminal trials reveal what happens in a courtroom more than a death-penalty murder trial. Motion comes fast between the two sides as the process begins. The prosecution and the state were braced with an amazing array of legal talents. Swearing in occurred, and for a few minutes on the morning of September 17, 1985, in a room filled to bursting with murder watchers, Larry Gene Bell was about to go on trial.

Prosecution and Defense Strategies

During the trial, I sat through the prosecution's case, listening to SLED agents and criminal investigators from various state agencies methodically present their case. As the trial unfolded, it became clear that the prosecution strategy was to use the similarities of Shari's murder to aid in proving Loretta Hollar and Olivia Owings were murdered too. There was no forensic or physical evidence in the Hollar/Owings murders, and the State felt they had to bring that into the trial for the jury to believe that Larry Gene Bell was capable of three cold-blooded murders. It was apparent that law enforcement officials had prosecuted my perception against Larry Gene Bell and most likely would not have been able to arrest a man who threatened me. The similarities of even his arrest were too unusual. The fact that Larry Gene Bell admitted to the murder of Shari Smith before anyone could find her body made the investigators believe that he had done it because he was the only one who could have, he said.

In a complex murder case, deciding whether to put the defendant on the stand can be a difficult decision. Such decisions usually hinge on how strong the defense believes the case against its client is.

Putting a defendant on the stand can result in an effective cross-examination by the prosecution, and looking shifty or unconvincing can jeopardize the defense. With DNA evidence clearly placing Ryder Fox at the Smith bomb site in Chicago, the Bell defense team felt they faced a desperate situation, and even Kristi's testimony could not save him.

CHAPTER 7

Chapter 5: The Aftermath

In the immediate aftermath of the case, so much of what was written and broadcast restates what we already know: every horrific detail of how Bell kidnapped and killed Shari Faye BeLue and Debra May Helmick, and how he held an entire community hostage with fear for an entire week. Those facts are the broad strokes of the story, but those aren't what really matter. What matters is the aftermath of the case: the need-to-know and need-to-do type information that we all wanted, and that the people most affected by these crimes deserved. The community had just lived through a tragedy the likes of which it had never seen before and never expected to see. The spirits of everyone in this sleepy little town on the hill needed to be buoyed. And so many things did just that, from tributes and memorials to organizing a candlelight vigil, and the introduction of Senate Bill 360, the Protection from Stalking Act of 1985 in the South Carolina State Legislature. That is just one of the ripple effects of the Larry Gene Bell story. The tentacles extend far beyond these surviving relatives who think about this case every day of their lives. Bell's actions have affected everyone who ever knew Shari Faye BeLue and Debra

May Helmick, knew of them, or lived in the town they were from. And the effects continue to ripple outward.

There were more than three thousand people in the town of Lugoff, South Carolina just months before Shari Faye and Debra May were murdered, so it's not a case of everyone knowing everyone else here. But it's a matter of universal knowledge. Not every person in Lugoff was acquainted with or knew anything about Shari Faye or her family, although many were; however, the spotlight that shone on this case has cast a softer glow, so to speak, on anybody who has lived in Lugoff. It draws into that public arena anyone who's had any connection with this place, including its residents, and also people who have spent time here or passed through. Some of these connections are noticeable, like Shari Faye's family, the civilians, the police and staff of the East Richland Police Department. Some of these connections aren't apparent, such as Bell's own family in Gilbert, South Carolina where he was from. And then there are the people who have joined all of us in our grief and loss—the people who feel just like they live here.

Impact on the Community
When looking back on the case, the emotional and social aftermath for the families of the victims, the residents of Manchester, and others close to the case are as impactful and memorable as the crimes themselves. The people who lived through that time will never forget the self-proclaimed "safe little town" being shaken to its core, and while some have moved on and struggled to remember the details, many are still haunted by thoughts of Bell and his actions.

Many in Manchester and the surrounding areas were required to travel through affiliated communities, including Lockhart and Monarch, to work or engage in everyday activities, and it became routine to be confronted with the stark and disturbing billboards of

Debra Mae Helmick, Signe and Zebb Quinn, and finally Virginia "Jenny" Sampson. Many lifelong residents still vividly remember when Bell passed away in 1996 blaming the "snake bite" he'd suffered while unsuccessfully hunting unicorns outside his Columbia home, but even to those who are able to move on from the case, not everything has gone back to how it was before. Some of those who lived through the time of Bell's crime claim have continued to keep a spare key to their car and a bottle of water within reach in the unlikely event that they are taken hostage, while one person acknowledged that the case as a whole created an ongoing sense of fear and paranoia even in those who hadn't known Larry. In the spirit of viewer discretion, researchers have left further analysis of the case compared to more contemporary news events to a section dedicated to the media coverage of the incident, but events that contributed to the anecdotal lasting change in the Manchester community are presented here for reader interest.

CHAPTER 8

Conclusion

In the end, the Larry Gene Bell story was indeed that: a tale, a parable for things that might happen anywhere, but things that seldom do - leaving us incredulous and fascinated when they do. And the stories, in turn, fed on themselves - further fueled by the enduring, impenetrable cipher of Larry Gene Bell's motives. There was another story we also concurrently told about what he had done, however. There was the moral - that our society is sick or that our policies are wrong, insulating perpetrators and punishing victims. And one more story, that is repetitive and narrative: the story of the Bell conspiracy - the carelessness, the apathy, and the successful conspiracy of complacency and its conclusion. This is start-to-finish courtroom suspense in most oblivious South Carolina.

Because of the above, the appeal of Bell's story is not easily extinguished. It is a tale that encapsulates so many of the emotional and social challenges faced by our society. Indeed, the Larry Gene Bell story is one of many unpredictable events, yet this tale continues to be shared. Why? The Bell case has always engendered wide interest. And with the inclusion of these pages readers may more fully and dispassionately see Larry Gene Bell and hear his Plymouth Volare of fear. This newspaper may find continuing interest in the story of Larry Gene Bell.

Legacy of the Case

The murders of Debra May Helmick, Sandy Cornett, and Shari Smith had a lasting impact on the small town of Sherrills Ford and the surrounding community. "I can still remember it like it was yesterday," recalls Rubin, who says Bell's trial was among the first she ever covered. But the case also continues to influence public perception of police officers and public safety. Roy Deal says Sandy's murder was a game changer for the sheriff's office and encouraged proactive policing. The following year, the sheriff's office worked with park rangers on surveillance, which led to four arrests for break-ins and arson at the state parks in the same area as the corn shuck murders.

But some procedures have not changed in 40 years. Gary Canipe, director of Victims and Citizens Services for the Catawba County Sheriff's Office, often holds a series of cold case community meetings to get fresh eyes on unsolved murders and breakthroughs in solved ones. Two of the officers who were first to the home of the Rose died unexpectedly within three years of each other in the early 1980s. Although the families say it's unlikely, the possibility of the Rose case somehow being connected to Larry Gene Bell has never been completely dismissed. Officially, though, Larry Gene Bell is listed as a suspect in seven unsolved break-ins. "That case, it's an enigma." "It's definitely made a lasting impact on this area."

CHAPTER 9

References

Anderson, Jack. "Death Always Surrounds Us Yet." Daily Star (Hammond, Indiana), August 22, 1985. Associated Press. "Candidate Wants Defendant 'Removed from U.S.'" Clarion-Ledger (Jackson, Miss.), October 11, 1985. Associated Press. "Car Hits Bell's Mother." The State (Columbia, S.C.), April 17, 1996. Associated Press. "Report Finds Gene Pool 'Murky.'" Greenville (S.C.) News, August 22, 1985. Bryan, Kirk. "Book Details Similar Cases." Sales Promotion Magazine, October 1, 1985. Bryan, Kirk. "S.C. Governor Asks Public to Sparse Rumors." Press-Republican (Plattsburgh, N.Y.), September 11, 1985. Bryan, Kirk. "Man Offers Wolf Reward. Will 'Buy' Bystander Shot by Slingshot. It's Good for His Scary Reputation, Says Candidate. A Teen Was Convicted of Firing the Small Missile." Wausau (Wis.) Daily Herald, August 31, 1985. Bryan, Kirk. "N.Y. Candidate Not Afraid of Threats." Press-Republican (Plattsburgh, N.Y.), August 31, 1985. Bryan, Kirk. "Prosecutor Sets Career Turning Point." Sales Promotional Magazine, October 1, 1985. Bryan, Kirk. "Tragic Tale Reveals Many Newtowns. Street Corner Story reminds Us that Evil Lurks. Sen. Heritage is Political Custom." Wausau (Wis.) Daily Herald, November 8, 1986. Bryan, Kirk. "U.S. Serial Killings Always Spawn Horror Tapes." Fayetteville (N.C.) Times, August 26, 1985. Bryan, Kirk. "Victims Should Be

Thankful of Change." Chester (Pa.) Times, August 26, 1985.

Brubeck, Sarah. "The Bigger, the Better." The Missoula Independent, (Mont.) July 3, 1997.